DATE			

LETTERS HOME
from
YOSEMITE

Lisa Halvorsen

BLACKBIRCH PRESS, INC.

WOODBRIDGE, CONNECTICUT

Published by Blackbirch Press, Inc.
260 Amity Road
Woodbridge, CT 06525

©2000 by Blackbirch Press, Inc.
First Edition

e-mail: staff@blackbirch.com
Web site: www.blackbirch.com

Printed in Singapore

10 9 8 7 6 5 4 3 2 1

All photographs ©Corel Corporation

Library of Congress Cataloging-in-Publication Data
Halvorsen, Lisa.
Yosemite / by Lisa Halvorsen.
　　p.　　cm. — (Letters home from national parks)
Includes bibliographical references and index.
Summary: This first-person account of a trip to Yosemite describes some of its outstanding fea-
tures including giant sequoias, Glacier Point, Cathedral Range, Tenaya Lake, and Tioga Pass.
ISBN 1-56711-462-8
1. Yosemite National Park (Calif.)—Juvenile literature. [1. Yosemite National Park (Calif.)
2. National parks and reserves] I. Title.
F868.Y6 .H19　2000
979.4'47—dc21
99-044255
CIP
AC

TABLE OF CONTENTS

Arrival in . . .

San Francisco

As our plane touched down in San Francisco, I knew we were in for an exciting vacation. I'd been reading about Yosemite on the plane. I learned that it is America's third national park. Yosemite is known throughout the world for its amazing scenery. It has incredible waterfalls, rock formations, alpine lakes and meadows, and giant sequoia trees. It's located in the east central part of California and covers 1,170 square miles. That's an area about the size of Rhode Island!

Efforts to protect the wilderness around Yosemite began in 1864. That's when President Abraham Lincoln signed the Yosemite Grant deeding the land to California. Yosemite was finally established as a national park on Oct. 1, 1890 by an act of Congress.

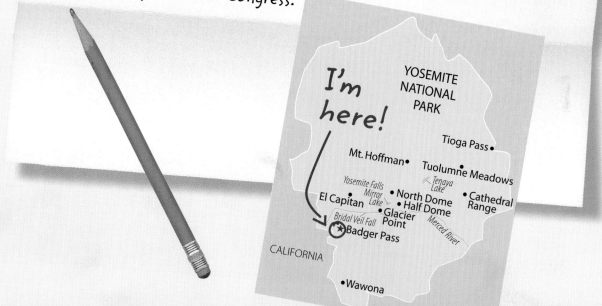

I'm here!

YOSEMITE NATIONAL PARK

Tioga Pass

Mt. Hoffman
Tuolumne Meadows

Yosemite Falls
Mirror Lake
Tenaya Lake
El Capitan
North Dome
Half Dome
Cathedral Range

Bridal Veil Fall
Glacier Point
Merced River

Badger Pass

CALIFORNIA

Wawona

Topography

Our tour guide said that one of the first people to visit this area was John Muir, a Scottish naturalist. He fought hard to convince the U. S. government to preserve Yosemite as a national park. The name supposedly comes from the Indian name "yo'hem-iteh." That means grizzly bear.

Yosemite is right in the middle of the Sierra Nevada Mountains. These mountains stretch for 430 miles along California's eastern border. The area covers 15.5 million acres, which is about the size of Vermont, New Hampshire, and Connecticut combined! This is the highest and longest single continuous range of mountains in the lower 48 states (not including Alaska and Hawaii).

Sierra Nevada

Sierra Nevada, from east of Tioga pass

Our guide said the range began to develop about 100 million years ago. Molten rock from deep inside the Earth combined with sediment on the ocean floor to form granite. Activity under the Earth's crust 10 million years ago pushed this block of granite upward to create a mountain range.

Later, during the Ice Age, glaciers widened and deepened the river canyons into U-shaped valleys. When the glaciers melted, the moraine (rock debris) that was left behind dammed up what is now Yosemite Valley.

Native Americans were the first people to live in Yosemite, about 7,000 to 10,000 years ago. When explorers arrived at Yosemite Valley in the 1830s and 1840s, Southern Sierra Miwok Indians were living there. They called the Yosemite Valley "Ahwahnee" (Place of the Gaping Mouth).

Badger Pass

The first tourists arrived in 1855. They traveled on horseback. I wonder if they were as amazed as I am by the first glimpse of this scenic park? Today, more than 3.5 million people visit the park every year. Most come in the summer months. That's a lot of visitors! And a lot of cars! But what's nice is that 94% of the park has been designated as wilderness. These areas can only be reached by foot or on horseback.

Merced River

Mist trail along the Merced River

Rafting on the Merced River

After a four-hour drive from San Francisco, we arrived at the Arch Rock entrance station. This is on the western side of the park, just north of Badger Pass. Badger is a popular ski spot. It opened in 1935 and was California's first ski area. Seven years earlier, the first ski school in the state was started in Yosemite Valley. That's where we'll begin exploring the park.

Yosemite Valley

Yosemite Valley is only seven miles long and one mile wide, but it's where the most services are. Our campground is here, and so are many of the park's best natural attractions. It's the most heavily visited part of the park.

Today, we learned about the Miwok and Paiute people, and about the natural history of the park. Then we hopped on the shuttle bus to see famous sights like Yosemite Falls, El Capitan, and Happy Isles. One of my favorite places was Mirror Lake, where we saw Tenaya Canyon reflected in the water.

Yosemite Valley

Pines and glacial debris

Setting sun in valley

Yosemite Valley

The ranger told us about Tunnel View, at the east end of the valley. What a sight! We could see El Capitan, Half Dome, Sentinel Rock, Cathedral Rocks, and Bridal Veil Fall. Many of these park landmarks can also be seen from the middle of the Swinging Bridge, which is a walkway over the Merced River. The Merced is one of two major park rivers. The other is the Tuolumne River. Yosemite also has more than 1,300 miles of streams and 600 lakes.

Later, we floated down the Merced River on inner tubes. It was almost 100 degrees Farenheit. That's hot even for Yosemite! Temperatures in winter range from the mid-20s to the high 40s. It can snow as early as September and as late as June. Some snow stays on the highest peaks year round.

Bridal Veil Creek/Fall

It seems that wherever we look, there's something bigger, higher, or more impressive than before. More than half of America's highest waterfalls are found in Yosemite. One of the prettiest is Bridal Veil Fall. It is located near the entrance to Yosemite Valley.

The Ahwahneechee called Bridal Veil Fall "Pohono." It means "spirit of the puffing wind." Sometimes hard winds actually blow the falls sideways! I'm glad I brought my raincoat because we got soaked by the spray on the way up! This waterfall is 620 feet high. That's as tall as a 62-story building!

Bridal Veil Fall and Merced River

Bridal Veil Creek

Some friends we met at the waterfall told us about their hike on the Mist Trail along the Merced River yesterday. They went to see two other popular waterfalls, Vernal and Nevada Falls.

You can view Vernal Falls from an observation bridge about a half mile from the trailhead. But most people walk right up to the falls. There are steps carved into the stone! Nevada Falls has an almost 600-foot drop. It's farther up the trail, which is often slippery because of mist from the river.

Yosemite/Sierra Plants and Trees

Thirty-seven different native trees grow in the park, from the giant sequoia to different species of oak, cedar, and pine. The California black oak is common. It was a source of food for the Ahwahneechee and many animals, including the acorn woodpecker. The native people ground the acorns into a flour to use in cooking. They also traded the acorns with the Paiute Indians for rabbit skins, pine nuts, obsidian (a volcanic glass black rock), and other things they couldn't find in the Yosemite Valley.

Little Yosemite Valley snowplant

Cedar, pine, and oak trees

Wildflowers

Bristlecone pine

Jeffery pine on Sentinel Dome

Some of the native tree species found in the river canyons include the incense cedar, which grows up to 150 feet tall; the California bay tree, with its spicy scent; the California nutmeg; and the California buck-eye. The buck-eye is one of the first trees to have leaves in the spring. Buckbrush, manzanita, and other types of chaparral (evergreen shrub) grow well on the steep, dry canyon walls.

Did you know that more than 1,400 kinds of flowers are found in the park? There are blue lupines, yellow seep-spring monkeyflowers, pink shooting stars, orange California poppies, and white mariposa tulips.

Giant Sequoias

I saw a Grizzly Giant! No, it's not a huge person. It's an enormous sequoia tree! It's the largest species of tree in the world and it is found only on the western slopes of the Sierra Nevada Mountains. A sequoia tree can grow to over 300 feet tall and 40 feet around, and can live more than 3,000 years! At about 2,700 years old, The Grizzly Giant is the oldest tree in the park and the fifth-oldest in the world. Many of the sequoias have nicknames, like the Clothespin Tree, Siamese Twins, and the Dead Giant. You can even walk through some of them!

Grizzly Giant in Mariposa grove

Mariposa grove of sequoia trees

Budding sitka spruce

Bark of ancient redwood trees

There are three groves of sequoias in the park. The largest is the Mariposa Grove. It is located by the southern entrance of Yosemite near Wawona. This is where the Grizzly Giant and the Fallen Tunnel Tree are located.

Merced Grove, which contains only 20 trees, is located in the Crane Flat area. This is 16 miles northwest of Yosemite Valley. You need to wear your hiking boots to see this group of trees. It's a four-mile round trip hike. The third stand of sequoias is called Tuolumne Grove. The starting point for a walk to this grove is also near Crane Flat.

Yosemite Wildlife

I'm so excited! This morning on our way to Glacier Point we saw a black bear and her two cubs. The young ones were as cute as teddy bears. The ranger reminded us how dangerous these bears really are. They have a very strong sense of smell and will rip open a tent or even break into a car to get food! That's why we put all our food—and even our toothpaste—in the bear-proof metal box at the campground.

An adult black bear can weigh as much as 500 pounds. The average size is about 300 pounds. Not all of them are black. They may be brown, cinnamon, or sometimes tan. Between 300 to 500 bears live in the park.

Black bear

Bobcat

We have seen a ton of mule deer since we arrived. They like to graze along the roadsides and in the meadows in the early morning and late afternoon. They can be just as aggressive as bears when approached. Mule deer have long ears like mules. They can run up to 35 miles an hour and can jump 24 feet in a single leap. You'd never know it from looking at them!

The park is also home to mountain lions, bobcats, coyotes, black-tailed jackrabbits, yellow-bellied marmots, rattlesnakes, and California bighorn sheep. Thousands of sheep once roamed the slopes of the Sierra Nevada Mountains. They were nearly wiped out by hunters, disease, and lack of food. A ranger said they were successfully reintroduced to the park in 1986.

Yosemite Wildlife

More than 240 species of birds have been spotted in Yosemite. Some of them are endangered, like the willow flycatcher and the great gray owl. Some—like the bald eagle—just spend the winter in the park. My favorite is the Steller's jay, a noisy blue bird with a black crest. It will steal food off your plate if you don't watch out!

I also like to watch bats swooping through the air to catch insects. Did you know that one bat can eat up to 600 mosquito-sized insects in an hour? Yosemite has 15 species of bats. These include the rare spotted bat, which has big ears and three white spots on its back.

Red-winged blackbird

Coyote howling

Glacier Point

The view from Glacier Point was totally awesome. It made me dizzy to look over the edge. It's 3,200 feet—a little more than a 1/2 mile—straight down to the floor of Yosemite Valley! In the distance I could see Yosemite Falls. I could also see El Capitan and Half Dome. I liked the way light reflected off the bare rock surfaces at sunrise and sunset, "painting" them pink, purple, and gold.

The ranger told us that this is a good place to see peregrine falcons in flight. They can dive at speeds up to 200 miles per hour and catch their prey in mid-air. They nest in high places on very narrow rock ledges.

Glacier Point

Sunset from Glacier Point Road

El Capitan

El Capitan is Spanish for "the Captain." This is the biggest single block of granite on Earth. It is more than 3,600 feet from its base to its top. It's a favorite climbing spot for visitors from all over the world. It can take anywhere from several hours to several days to scale this rock. So it's not unusual to see people camped out on the rock ledges.

The highest single waterfall on the North American continent is Ribbon Fall. It plunges 1,612 feet off a cliff on the west side of El Capitan.

El Capitan

Sunrise over El Capitan

Yosemite Falls

All together, Yosemite Falls are the highest waterfalls in North America and rank number five in the world. There are actually three sections of falls, one on top of the other. The total drop is 2,425 feet, which is as high as 13 Niagara Falls!

In late spring and early summer, so much water goes over the falls that you can feel the ground shake! By the end of the summer, the falls may be no more than a trickle. And some years they dry up all together.

Yosemite Creek near top of Yosemite Falls

Yosemite Falls

Half Dome

Half Dome is one of the most recognizable landmarks in Yosemite. That's because it looks like half a loaf of bread! Geologists say it is around 87 million years old. Its other half probably broke off when the glaciers receded many thousands of years ago.

Some people say that if you look very carefully you can see a profile of an Ahwahneechee Indian princess on the face of the dome. As hard as I tried, I couldn't find the princess. But I did spot a pair of golden eagles making circles in the sky.

Sunset—
Half Dome

Half
Dome

North Dome

Opposite Half Dome, along the north wall of Tenaya Canyon, is another large granite rock called North Dome. It's slightly smaller than Half Dome but just as awesome. If you look up about 1,500 feet from the valley floor, you can see the Royal Arches. This interesting geological formation was the work of a glacier.

The domes occur mostly on the western slopes of the Sierra Nevada. Their smooth, rounded shape is due to something called exfoliation. That's a process that peels away rock layers, like the skin of an onion.

North Dome

Cathedral Range

We learned about some of the smaller mountain ranges in the Sierra Nevadas at the park ranger's program last night. One is the Cathedral Range, which includes the 10,940-foot Cathedral Peak and 11,780-foot Parsons Peak. Cathedral Peak, a favorite with climbers, gets its name from its shape. It really does look like a church with a tall steeple!

In the late 19th century, a few mining companies operated in this part of the park. But instead of looking for gold, miners tunneled through the rock in hopes of finding rich veins of silver.

Cathedral Range

Mt. Hoffman

Wildflowers

The Tioga Road, which crosses the Cathedral Range, was originally a wagon road. It was built in 1883 by Chinese workers for the Great Sierra Consolidated Silver Company for the purpose of hauling ore. The road was later paved and widened. It is now one of the most scenic routes through the park. While traveling on this road, we stopped at May Lake. We took lots of pictures of Mt. Hoffman and gazed at its reflection in the lake. I read in my guidebook that this mountain is in the geographic center of the park. At 10,850 feet high, it's one of the shorter peaks.

Lyell

The first person to climb Mt. Lyell was John Tileston in 1871. At 13,114 feet, Mt. Lyell is the park's highest mountain. It also has the largest active glacier, the Lyell Glacier, which clings to the northwest side of the peak. It is about 1/4 mile square. Melting snow from the glacier feeds the Tuolumne River. The river, in turn, provides water to San Francisco by way of a reservoir.

Today the rivers and streams of Yosemite provide places to fish, wade, or raft. But in the past, people flocked to the water to pan for gold! While some gold was found, the area did not yield as much of this precious metal as the foothills to the west of the park did.

Lyell Fork

Tenaya Lake

Today we went swimming in Tenaya Lake in the high country. Brrrr, was it cold! That's because the water comes from mountain streams.

The lake was named for the leader of the Yosemite tribe, Chief Tenaya. In 1851, soldiers captured him near here. They said he led a raid on a trading post in the Merced River Canyon. The Native Americans had their own name for the lake, "Pywiak." This means shining rocks. I like that name better. When the domes surrounding the lake are reflected in the water, it really does look like a lake of shining rocks!

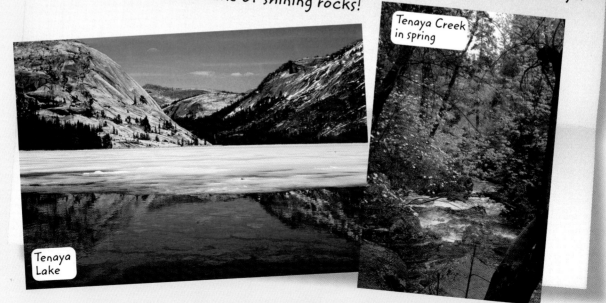

Tenaya Creek in spring

Tenaya Lake

Tuolumne Meadows

The Tuolumne meadows (elevation: 8,575 feet) are the largest meadows in the Sierra Nevada. It's also is a very popular place to camp. The views are breathtaking. There is nowhere else in the world with such a large concentration of domes. The largest dome is Fairview. It stands about 2,000 feet tall. The domes are popular with rock climbers. From here they look like spiders crawling up the sides of the rocks!

There are meadows covered with many short grasses including beaked sedges, tufted hairgrass, and shorthair reed grass. In the spring and summer the meadow is carpeted with wildflowers.

It's not as crowded here as it was in Yosemite Valley. It's also much cooler.

Wildflowers on Half Dome Trail

Tuolumne Meadows from Pothole Dome

Tioga Pass

On our last day we drove over Tioga Pass. It's 9,945 feet above sea level. It's the highest highway pass in the Sierra Nevada range and in all of California. Because it's so high, many flowers and plants that grow here differ from those in lower elevations such as the Yosemite Valley. The trees are also small and stunted, because it's difficult for them to grow at such high altitudes. Wherever you go—high in the mountains, or low in the valleys—Yosemite is truly one of the most awesome places on Earth!

Lake in Tioga Pass area

Juniper tree

Glossary

Endangered species a type of plant or animal that is in danger of dying out.

Exfoliation the peeling back of layers.

Glacier a huge sheet of ice found in a mountain valley or polar region.

Graze to feed off grass in a field.

Native someone or something that originally lived in a certain place.

Naturalist someone who studies animals and plants.

Reservoir holding area that stores a large amount of water.

Sediment rocks and particles that have been carried and deposited by glaciers.

For More Information

Books

Patent, Dorothy Hinshaw. William Munoz (Illustrator). *Places of Refuge: Our National Wildlife Refuge System.* New York, NY: Clarion Books, 1992.

Tesar, Jenny. *America's Top 10 National Parks (America's Top 10).* Woodbridge, CT: Blackbirch Press, Inc., 1998.

Video

Yosemite (Reader's Digest), 1993.

Web Sites

The History of Yosemite

Information on the exploration of the Yosemite Valley terraquest.com/highsights/valley/yoshist.html

Yosemite National Park

This offical web site provides detailed information about the park—www.nps.gov/yose

Index